1 3 5 7 9 10 8 6 4 2

Published in 2009 by BBC Books, an imprint of Ebury Publishing
A Random House Group company

The Random House Group Limited Reg. No. 954009

Addresses for companies within the Random House Group can be found at
www.randomhouse.co.uk

A CIP catalogue record for this book is available from the British Library.

The Random House Group Limited supports The Forest Stewardship Council (FSC), the leading international forest certification organization. All our titles that are printed on Greenpeace approved FSC certified paper carry the FSC logo. Our paper procurement policy can be found at www.rbooks.co.uk/environment

To buy books by your favourite authors and register for offers visit www.rbooks.co.uk

Printed and bound by Firmengruppe APPL, aprinta druck, Wemding, Germany
Colour origination by Dot Gradations Ltd, UK

Commissioning Editor: Muna Reyal
Project Editor: Laura Higginson
Designer: Kathryn Gammon
Production: Lucy Harrison
Picture Researcher: Gabby Harrington

ISBN: 978 184 607811 8

olive

101 STYLISH SUPPERS

Editor
Janine Ratcliffe

BOOKS

641.538

Contents

Introduction

At **olive** we believe it's easy to put together stylish dishes every night of the week without spending too much time in the kitchen or fussing over complicated recipes. Homecooking is more popular than ever now, not only because it saves money but also because it allows us to know exactly what goes into our food.

All the recipes chosen by the **olive** team for this book are imaginative, satisfying and, best of all, easy. So dishes like *Balsamic-glazed steak with garlicky green beans*, pictured opposite, are achievable but still smart enough for entertaining friends (see page 54 for the recipe).

There are recipes to suit every mood; so whether you are looking for a healthy salad, a comforting pasta supper or a show-off lamb dish, you'll find them all here.

As always, all the recipes have been thoroughly tested in the **olive** kitchen to make sure they taste fabulous and work for you first time. Eating out at home has never been easier!

Janine Ratcliffe

Janine Ratcliffe
Food Editor
olive magazine

Notes and Conversions

NOTES ON THE RECIPES

• Where possible, we use humanely reared meats, free-range chickens and eggs, and unrefined sugar.

• Eggs are large unless stated otherwise. Pregnant women, elderly people, babies and toddlers, and anyone who is unwell should avoid eating raw and partially cooked eggs.

APPROXIMATE WEIGHT CONVERSIONS

• All the recipes in this book are listed with metric measurements.

• Cup measurements, which are used by cooks in Australia and America, have not been listed here as they vary from ingredient to ingredient. Please use kitchen scales to measure dry/solid ingredients.

OVEN TEMPERATURES

gas	°C	fan °C	°F	description
¼	110	90	225	Very cool
½	120	100	250	Very cool
1	140	120	275	Cool or slow
2	150	130	300	Cool or slow
3	160	140	325	Warm
4	180	160	350	Moderate
5	190	170	375	Moderately hot
6	200	180	400	Fairly hot
7	220	200	425	Hot
8	230	210	450	Very hot
9	240	220	475	Very hot

SPOON MEASURES

Spoon measurements are level unless otherwise specified.

• 1 teaspoon (tsp) = 5ml
• 1 tablespoon (tbsp) = 15ml
• 1 Australian tablespoon = 20ml (cooks in Australia should measure 3 teaspoons where 1 tablespoon is specified in a recipe)

APPROXIMATE LIQUID CONVERSIONS

metric	imperial	US
60ml	2fl oz	$\frac{1}{4}$ cup
125ml	4fl oz	$\frac{1}{2}$ cup
175ml	6fl oz	$\frac{3}{4}$ cup
225ml	8fl oz	1 cup
300ml	10fl oz/$\frac{1}{2}$ pint	$1\frac{1}{4}$ cups
450ml	16fl oz	2 cups/1 pint
600ml	20fl oz/1 pint	$2\frac{1}{2}$ cups
1 litre	35fl oz/$1\frac{3}{4}$ pints	1 quart

Please note that an Australian cup is 250ml, $\frac{3}{4}$ cup is 190ml, $\frac{1}{2}$ cup is 125ml, $\frac{1}{4}$ cup is 60ml.

Rich tomato and thyme soup

30 minutes ■ Serves 4

onion 1, roughly chopped

garlic 2 cloves, crushed

carrot 1, diced

olive oil

thyme leaves from 2 sprigs

chicken or **vegetable stock** 750ml

plum tomatoes 2 x 400g tins

tomato purée 1 tbsp

half-fat crème fraîche 100g

■ Cook the onion, garlic and carrot in 1 tbsp oil until softened, about 5 minutes. Add the thyme, stock, tomatoes and tomato purée, and simmer for 15 minutes until slightly thickened. Pour into a blender and blend until smooth. Stir in the crème fraîche and serve.

Tinned plum tomatoes are brilliant to use when fresh tomatoes are out of season.

Pea soup with Parma ham croutons

20 minutes ■ Serves 6

onion 1 large, finely chopped

butter

chicken stock 1 litre

frozen petits pois 600g

tarragon or **parsley** small bunch, chopped

cream 142ml carton

bread sticks 12 very thin ones

Parma ham 6 slices, each halved lengthways

■ Fry the onion in a knob of butter until tender, add the stock, peas and tarragon or parsley and simmer for 3 minutes. Add the cream, blend to a smooth soup and season. Heat the oven to 180C/fan 160C/gas 4. Wrap each bread stick in a piece of ham and bake for 15 minutes or until the ham crisps. Serve with the soup.

For a veggie version, just substitute vegetable stock for the chicken and sprinkle the breadsticks with parmesan before baking.

Beef tataki salad

15 minutes ■ Serves 2

steak 1, about 200g, fat removed

rocket 50g bag

radishes 10, thinly sliced

red onion ½ small, thinly sliced

soy sauce 4 tbsp

lime 1, juiced

sesame oil 1 tbsp

caster sugar 1 tsp

sesame seeds tsp

■ Chargrill or grill the steak for about 2 minutes a side until medium−rare. Rest for 5 minutes. Arrange the rocket, radishes and red onion on 2 plates. Slice the steak and divide between the salads. Whisk the soy, lime, sesame oil and sugar and drizzle over the salads. Sprinkle with sesame seeds to finish.

You can use fillet, sirloin or rump steak for this, depending on your budget and what's available.

Thai noodle soup with coconut and salmon

20 minutes ■ Serves 2

Thai red curry paste 2 tbsp
light coconut milk 165ml tin
chicken stock 500ml
skinless salmon fillets 2, about 125g each
dried egg noodles 100g
fish sauce 1 tbsp
lime 1, juiced
spring onions 2, shredded
red chilli 1, shredded
coriander a few leaves, to serve (optional)

■ Heat a wide non-stick pan and cook the curry paste for a couple of minutes until fragrant. Add the coconut milk and stock and bring to a simmer. Simmer for 5 minutes then turn down the heat to low and add the salmon. Poach for 4–5 minutes until just cooked.

■ Cook the noodles according to the pack instructions, drain and divide between 2 soup bowls. Sit a salmon fillet on top of each stack of noodles. Add the fish sauce and lime juice to the soup and pour over the noodles. Top with the spring onions, chilli and coriander, if using.

Thai curry pastes vary in heat – add more or less to get the level you want.

Spicy tomato rasam soup

35 minutes ■ Serves 4

tomatoes 12 medium, quartered

garlic 3 cloves

root ginger 2.5cm, peeled and sliced

tamarind purée 100g

coriander a small bunch, finely chopped, reserve a few whole leaves to serve

green chilli 1 medium, slit lengthways

turmeric powder 1 tsp

ground coriander ½ tsp

vegetable oil

mustard seeds 1 tsp

dried red chillies 3 small, crushed or a pinch of chilli flakes

cumin seeds ½ tsp

naan bread, to serve

■ Put the tomatoes, garlic and ginger in a blender with 200ml water and blend for 1 minute or until smooth. Pour into a large pan and add the tamarind, fresh coriander, green chilli, turmeric, ground coriander and season. Bring to a boil and cook on a medium heat for 25 minutes. If it's too thick, add a little more water.

■ Heat 3 tbsp oil in a small frying pan. Add the mustard seeds, and when they begin to pop, add the red chillies and cumin. Fry for 10 seconds then remove from the heat.

■ Pour the soup into bowls and spoon the spice oil over each. Serve with fresh coriander leaves and naan bread.

The best thing about this soup is that almost no chopping is required. All the ingredients go into the blender or food processor and then straight into the pot.

Steak and chickpea salad with harissa yoghurt dressing

15 minutes ■ Serves 2

chickpeas 400g tin, drained and rinsed

red onion ½ small, sliced

cherry tomatoes 100g, halved

flat-leaf parsley a small bunch, chopped

sirloin steak about 200g, trimmed of all fat

natural yoghurt 150ml

harissa 2 tbsp

■ Toss together the chickpeas, red onion, tomatoes and parsley. Season the steak well and cook for 1½ minutes each side, then rest for 5 minutes. Mix the yoghurt with the harissa and a splash of water.

■ Slice the steak, toss with the chickpeas and serve drizzled with the yoghurt.

Harissa is a Moroccan spice blend, usually sold as a paste in a jar or tube. Find it next to the spices in supermarkets and grocers.

Sweet chilli salmon and warm rice salad

20 minutes ■ Serves 2

salmon 2 skinless fillets

sweet chilli sauce 3 tbsp

lime 1, ½ juiced, ½ cut into wedges

basmati rice 100g

white wine vinegar 2 tbsp

golden caster sugar 1 tbsp

carrot 1 large, julienned

spring onions 2, shredded

red chilli 1, shredded

■ Put the salmon with the chilli sauce and lime juice in a plastic bag and marinate for 10 minutes. Cook the rice and drain. Whisk the vinegar and sugar and toss with the rice while warm.

■ Grill the salmon for 4–5 minutes until just cooked through. Flake the salmon into chunks. Toss the carrot, spring onions and chilli with the rice, gently stir through the salmon and serve.

This also works with hot chilli sauce if you want to turn up the heat a bit.

Prawn and avocado salad with coconut dressing

20 minutes ■ Serves 2

vermicelli rice noodles 100g

coconut milk 4 tbsp

lime ½, juiced

chives 1 tbsp, chopped

root ginger a thumb-sized piece, finely grated

cooked peeled prawns 100g

avocado 1, peeled and sliced

■ Soak the rice noodles in boiling water until just tender.

■ Drain and rinse under cold water then drain again. Whisk the coconut milk, lime juice, chives and ginger to make a dressing. Toss with the prawns, avocado and noodles, season with salt and serve.

Freeze the rest of the coconut milk to use in soups and curries.

Thai chicken salad

20 minutes ■ Serves 4

minced chicken or **turkey** 400g

chicken stock 100ml

root ginger a thumb-sized piece, grated

garlic 2 cloves, finely chopped

lemon grass 1 stalk, woody outer leaves removed, finely chopped

red chillies 2, finely chopped

fish sauce 2 tbsp

lime juice 3 tbsp

mint and **coriander** leaves, a small handful of each

little gem lettuce leaves and **cucumber batons** to serve

■ Cook the chicken or turkey in the stock in a frying pan until it turns white and the stock evaporates. Add the ginger, garlic, lemon grass and chillies and keep cooking for another 3 minutes. Take off the heat and stir in the fish sauce and lime juice. Stir in the herbs and serve with lettuce leaves and cucumber batons.

If you can't find chicken mince just whizz chopped chicken thighs to mince in a food processor.

Hot and sour watercress and prawn broth

10 minutes ■ Serves 2

rice vinegar or **white wine vinegar** 3 tbsp

vegetable or **chicken stock** 500ml

soy sauce 1 tbsp

golden caster sugar 1–2 tsp

root ginger 2.5cm piece, peeled and thinly sliced

red chillies 2 small hot ones, thinly sliced

spring onions 3, thinly sliced

raw peeled prawns 300g

watercress 1 bunch or bag

■ Put the vinegar, stock, soy sauce, sugar (start with 1 tsp and add the second at the end if you want the soup sweeter), ginger, chillies and spring onions in a pan and bring to a simmer.

■ Cook for a minute then add the prawns and cook until they turn pink. Stir in the watercress and turn off the heat. Taste and add more sugar, if you like.

Remove the big woody stalks from the watercress, as these won't be good in the soup.

Thai sweetcorn soup

20 minutes ■ Serves 4

Thai red curry paste 1 tbsp
coconut milk 400ml tin
sweetcorn sliced off the cob to make 200g
cherry tomatoes 16, halved
raw peeled prawns from a sustainable source 200g
chicken or **vegetable stock** 500ml
coriander a small bunch, roughly chopped

■ Heat the red curry paste in a pan until it starts to sizzle in its own oil, stir in the coconut milk and bring to a simmer. Add the corn and cook for 3 minutes, then add the cherry tomatoes and prawns and cook for a minute. Add the stock and stir well, then stir in the coriander.

Add some rice or noodles to this soup if you want to make it more substantial.

Asian turkey soup

20 minutes ■ Serves 2

red chilli 1, shredded

shallots 2, peeled and quartered

chicken stock 500ml

rice or **cider vinegar** 2 tbsp

soy sauce 1 tbsp

spring onions ½ bunch, sliced

cooked turkey 2 or 3 large slices, chopped
or shredded

coriander ½ pack, roughly chopped

rice vermicelli 100g, cooked (optional)

■ Put the chilli and shallots in a pan with the stock, bring to a simmer and cook for 3 minutes. Add the vinegar and soy sauce. Taste and add more vinegar if you want more of a sour flavour. Add the spring onions and cook for a minute, then add the turkey and cook for another minute. Stir in the coriander and spoon over the noodles (if using) to serve.

This is a great way to use up cooked leftovers, you could also make it with pork, chicken or beef.

Bulgar wheat, feta and broccoli salad

30 minutes ■ Serves 2

bulgar wheat 75g

Tenderstem broccoli tips 125g

lemon 1, juiced

olive oil

garlic ½ clove, crushed

feta 100g

tomatoes 2, diced

pine nuts 2 tbsp, toasted

flat-leaf parsley a small bunch, chopped

■ Tip the bulgar into a pan of salted boiling water. Take off the heat, cover and soak for 10–15 minutes. Drain well. Blanch the broccoli until just tender but still bright green. Toss the bulgar with all the other ingredients and season.

Bulgar wheat is a cracked, part-cooked grain, which is brilliant at absorbing other flavours.

Beetroot, green bean and goat's cheese salad

15 minutes ■ Serves 2

olive oil

red wine vinegar 1 tbsp

orange 1 tbsp juice and zest of ½

shallot 1, very finely chopped

wholegrain mustard 2 tsp

green beans 200g, blanched and drained

cooked beetroot 4 small, cut into wedges

goat's cheese 100g, crumbled

■ To make a dressing, whisk 3 tbsp olive oil, the vinegar, orange juice and zest, shallot and mustard together and season. Toss three-quarters of dressing with the beans.

■ Arrange the beans, beetroot and cheese on 2 plates and drizzle over extra dressing.

Look for vac-packed cooked beetroot rather than the stuff in vinegar.

French bean and chorizo salad

30 minutes ■ Serves 4

shallots 2 large or 4 small, finely chopped
sherry vinegar or **white wine vinegar**
2 tbsp
French beans 300g, tails cut off
blanched almonds 100g
butter
chorizo 100g, halved and sliced (pull off the outer skin if you need to)
parsley a handful, roughly chopped

■ Put the shallots and vinegar in a small bowl and leave to soak. Steam or simmer the beans until tender, about 4 minutes. Cool under running water and drain. Put the beans on a large platter.

■ Heat a frying pan and add the almonds and a knob of butter, cook, stirring until the almonds brown, salt well, and tip over the beans. Fry the chorizo until it begins to brown and give off oil. Drain the oil and tip the chorizo onto the beans. Add the shallots and parsley, season with pepper and toss everything together.

French or green beans give this salad a lovely texture, but you could also use runner beans when in season.

Peach, prosciutto and mozzarella salad

15 minutes ■ Serves 2

peaches 2 ripe, stoned and quartered

prosciutto 4 slices, torn

mozzarella 1 ball, torn into pieces

rocket 2 handfuls

olive oil 2 tbsp

lemon juice 1 tbsp

maple syrup ½ tbsp

pine nuts 2 tbsp, toasted

■ Arrange the peaches, prosciutto, mozzarella and rocket on 2 plates. Whisk the olive oil, lemon juice, and maple syrup. Drizzle the dressing over and scatter the pine nuts on top.

Other juicy, sweet fruit such as melon or figs would also work well instead of the peaches.

New potato, trout and lemon herb salad

20 minutes ■ Serves 2

small new potatoes 250g, halved

lemon 1, juiced

spring onions 2, sliced

dill a small bunch, chopped

watercress 50g

hot-smoked trout 125g, flaked

■ Cook the potatoes until just tender. Drain and cool a little. Mix the lemon juice, spring onions and dill and toss with the potatoes. Carefully fold through the watercress and trout and serve.

Hot-smoked trout is cooked rather than cured so it has a meatier texture than cold smoked.

Red quinoa, feta and spinach salad

25 minutes ■ Serves 4

red quinoa 200g, buy from healthfood shops and larger supermarkets (or use ordinary quinoa)

olive oil

red wine vinegar 2 tbsp

garlic 1 clove, crushed

ground cumin 2 tsp

feta 200g block, crumbled

cucumber ½, chopped

spinach 150g, roughly chopped

spring onions 4, shredded

■ Cook the quinoa according to the pack instructions. Drain well then toss with 2 tbsp oil, the vinegar, garlic and cumin while still warm and season. Toss through the rest of the ingredients and serve.

Try using goat's cheese or halloumi instead of the feta.

Spring chowder

15 minutes ■ Serves 4

onion 1 large, finely chopped
garlic 1 clove, crushed
olive oil
spring cabbage 500g, finely shredded
chicken or **vegetable stock** 1.5 litres
parsley 1 small bunch, chopped
feta 100g, crumbled

■ Fry the onion and garlic in olive oil until soft but not coloured – this will take about 5 minutes. Add the cabbage, stock and parsley and bring to a simmer, cook for 5 minutes or until the cabbage is soft. Season well. Serve in deep bowls with the feta stirred through.

Veg boxes always seem to include a cabbage, and spring cabbages such as primo make a good base for fresher flavoured ingredients like feta.

Potato and parmesan soup

30 minutes ■ Serves 2

onions 2, chopped

butter

potatoes 3, peeled and cut into chunks

vegetable stock 500ml

semi-skimmed milk 300ml

parmesan 25g, grated, plus a few shavings to serve

chives snipped to serve

■ Cook the onions in a knob of butter until soft. Add the potatoes, stock and milk and simmer until tender. Whizz in a blender until smooth, stir in the parmesan, season and top with chives and the parmesan shavings.

The thickness of the soup will depend on your potatoes – just add a little more stock after blending if you want it thinner.

Warm Puy lentil, cherry tomato and halloumi salad

30 minutes ■ Serves 4

cherry tomatoes 250g, halved

red onion ½, finely sliced

garlic ½ clove, crushed

lemon ½ juiced

olive oil 1 tbsp

Puy lentils 150g

halloumi 250g pack, cut into chunks

coriander a small bunch, roughly chopped

■ Toss the tomatoes, red onion, garlic, lemon juice and olive oil in a bowl. Cook the Puy lentils until just tender, drain and add to the bowl. Season well and toss. Grill the halloumi until golden. Stir the coriander through the lentils and serve with the halloumi.

Always add the lentils to the dressing while warm as this helps to soak up all the flavours.

Marinated courgette salad with pine nuts and parmesan

30 minutes ■ Serves 4

olive oil 3 tbsp

lemon juice 2 tbsp

shallots 2, finely chopped

red chilli 1, finely chopped

courgettes 4, cut into long ribbons with a potato peeler

pine nuts 4 tbsp, toasted

basil a handful of leaves, shredded

parmesan a handful of shavings to serve

■ Whisk the olive oil and lemon juice with the shallots and chilli. Toss the courgettes with the dressing and leave for 5 minutes. Toss with the pine nuts and basil then scatter with parmesan.

You can prepare the parts of this salad ahead, but toss just before serving otherwise the courgette will become too soggy.

Balsamic-glazed steak with garlicky green beans

30 minutes ■ Serves 2

olive oil

garlic 2 cloves, sliced

plum tomatoes 400g tin

cloves 4

green beans 150g

sirloin steaks 2, all fat trimmed off

balsamic vinegar 2 tbsp

■ Heat 1 tbsp olive oil in a pan. Add the garlic and sizzle for 2 minutes. Add the tomatoes and cloves and simmer for about 10 minutes until thickened. Fish out the cloves then add the beans with a splash of water and cook for 3–4 minutes until just tender.

■ Heat a frying pan until it's smoking hot. Season the steaks well then sear for 1 minute on each side. Add the balsamic to the pan and cook for another 30 seconds on each side. Rest for 3–4 minutes. Pile up the beans and sauce on 2 plates.

■ Thickly slice the steak and put on top of the beans.

For everyday cooking use a cheaper balsamic – keep the really good stuff for drizzling on salads or dipping bread.

Lamb cutlets with mint relish

45 minutes ■ Serves 4

new potatoes or **salad potatoes** 400g
olive oil
lamb cutlets 12
MINT RELISH
lemon 1, juiced
mint 1 bunch, finely chopped
sugar 2 tbsp
shallots 2, finely chopped

■ Heat the oven to 200C/fan 180C/gas 6. Cook the potatoes in simmering water for 8 minutes, drain and cool briefly.

■ Toss in a little olive oil and then tip into a shallow roasting tin, squash each one down so it splits, and season with salt. Roast for 20 minutes or until golden and crisp.

■ Meanwhile, mix the ingredients for the mint relish together, crushing the mint into the sugar. Set aside.

■ Brush the cutlets with olive oil and season well. Heat a frying pan and fry the cutlets on each side for 1 minute. Serve with the relish and potatoes.

The mint relish is also great with a traditional roast lamb leg.

Broad bean and bacon risotto

1 hour ■ Serves 4

chicken or **vegetable stock** 1.5 litres
broad beans 400g after double podding
(you'll need about 2kg to start)
butter 50g
onion 1, finely chopped
bacon 8 rashers, about 200g, finely sliced
garlic 1 clove, crushed
risotto rice 300g
white wine 1 glass
pecorino shaved or grated, to serve

■ Heat the stock in a pan and add the broad beans, cook for 3 minutes then scoop them out.

■ Melt a large knob of butter in a large pan and fry the onion and bacon for about 5 minutes until the onion is tender. Add the garlic and cook for a minute. Stir in the rice, coating every grain in butter.

■ Add the wine and stir until it has been absorbed, then add the stock a ladleful at a time, stirring until it has been absorbed but so that the risotto is still wet enough to just hold its shape. Season. Stir in another knob of butter and half of the broad beans.

■ Spoon the risotto into bowls and top with more broad beans and the pecorino.

Frozen broad beans will work just as well in this, you'll need about 1kg. Just blanch them briefly and squeeze out of their pods.

Fiorelli with broccoli and crisp prosciutto

15 minutes ■ Serves 2

fiorelli 150g

olive oil

garlic 1 clove, crushed

prosciutto 4 slices, shredded

Tenderstem broccoli tips 125g, blanched

parmesan to serve

■ Cook the fiorelli according to the pack instructions. Heat 3 tbsp olive oil and sizzle the garlic for a couple of minutes.

■ Add the prosciutto and sizzle until crisp. Toss with the pasta and broccoli and serve sprinkled with shavings of parmesan.

If you can't find fiorelli, just use any other short pasta shape for this.

Tenderstem broccoli and chorizo with poached eggs

20 minutes ■ Serves 2

chorizo 40g, cut into strips
red chilli ½ finely chopped
garlic clove 1, sliced
olive oil
Tenderstem broccoli 200g, sliced
eggs 2
red wine vinegar 2 tbsp

■ Gently cook the chorizo, chilli and garlic in 1 tbsp olive oil for a few minutes. Blanch the Tenderstem broccoli until just tender, about 2–3 minutes. Poach the eggs until the whites are set but the yolks are still runny.

■ Add the red wine vinegar to the chorizo pan and bubble for 30 seconds, then toss with the cooked broccoli.

■ Arrange on warm plates and top with a poached egg to serve.

You can also serve this as a cold salad with boiled eggs instead of poached.

Lamb and spinach pilaf

30 minutes ■ Serves 4

olive oil

lamb leg steaks 2, cut into chunks

onion 1, sliced

garlic 2 cloves, crushed

cumin seeds 1 tsp

cardamom pods 4, lightly crushed

basmati rice 300g

chicken stock 550ml

spinach 100g, washed and chopped

■ Heat 1 tbsp olive oil in a pan, add the lamb and brown quickly all over. Add the onion and garlic and cook for 5 minutes until softened, then stir in the spices and rice. Pour over the stock, bring to a simmer and cover with a tight-fitting lid. Turn the heat down and cook gently until all the stock has been absorbed, about 15 minutes. Stir through the spinach for the last minute of cooking until wilted.

Lamb leg is great for quick dishes as it doesn't need lengthy cooking to become tender.

Vietnamese lemon grass beef platter

45 minutes ■ Serves 4

fillet steak 500g, thinly sliced
lemon grass 4 stalks, woody outer leaves removed, chopped
garlic 4 cloves, finely chopped
red chilli 1 small, deseeded and chopped
shallots 2, finely chopped
fish sauce 2 tbsp
vegetable oil
ACCOMPANIMENTS
rice vermicelli noodles 150g
cos or **baby gem lettuce** 12 crisp leaves
coriander, **mint**, **dill** and **basil leaves**
carrots or **cucumbers** julienned
fried onion, **garlic** or **shallot** slices
spring onions, sliced
chilli dipping sauce

■ Soak some wooden skewers for 15 minutes or use metal ones. Thread the beef onto the skewers then put in a flat dish and marinate in the lemon grass, garlic, chilli, shallots, fish sauce and 2 tsp oil for at least 15 minutes. Chill until ready to cook.

■ For the accompaniments, pour boiling water over the noodles and soak until al dente. Drain, rinse in cold water and dry on tea towels. Cut into shorter pieces with scissors and drizzle a little oil over to keep from sticking. Put on platters with the other fresh herbs and vegetables. Keep refrigerated.

■ Heat a grill pan, barbecue or frying pan. Brown the meat in batches for a minute on each side. Serve with accompaniments and sauce.

Arrange all the accompaniments on a platter and let your guests help themselves. Crispy fried onions are a nice finishing touch and Asian shops sell them in little jars.

Crisp pork in lettuce cups with chilli lime sauce

20 minutes ■ Serves 4

lemon grass 4 stalks, woody outer leaves removed
vegetable oil
lean minced pork 400g
palm or **soft brown sugar** 1 tbsp
red onion 1 small, finely chopped
coriander a small bunch, chopped (keep some leaves for decoration)
baby gem lettuce 4, chilled and leaves separated
CHILLI LIME SAUCE
garlic 1 clove, finely chopped
red chilli 1 small, deseeded and finely chopped
palm sugar or **soft brown sugar** 1 tbsp
limes 3, juiced
fish sauce 1 tbsp

■ Slice off the hard bottom and top third of the lemon grass and finely chop the soft inner part. Heat a wok or large pan with 2 tbsp oil. Add the lemon grass and fry until soft for about 2 minutes. Add the minced pork and let it go brown and crisp on the bottom before breaking up with a spoon. Cook through thoroughly, add the sugar, stir again then take off the heat.

■ To make the sauce, crush the garlic, chilli and sugar to a paste with a mortar and pestle. Add the lime juice and fish sauce and pound until mixed, or you can put the garlic, chilli, sugar, lime juice and fish sauce in a small jar and shake well to dissolve the sugar.

■ Pour the dressing over the warm pork along with the onion and coriander. Gently stir and serve with the chilled baby gem lettuce to scoop up bites with. Sprinkle with more fresh coriander.

This quick dish is based on a Thai dish called larb (a meat salad), and is an impressive one to throw together for friends.

Pappardelle with sausage, fennel and red wine

30 minutes ■ Serves 4

olive oil

pork sausages 6, skinned

fennel seeds 1 tsp

garlic 1 clove, sliced

red wine a large glass

chopped tomatoes 400g tin

pappardelle 300g

■ Heat 2 tbsp olive oil in a large, wide, non-stick pan. Pinch off little nuggets of sausage into the pan then fry until browned.

■ Add the fennel seeds and garlic and cook for a minute. Add the red wine and let it bubble up fiercely for a couple of minutes then tip in the tomatoes. Simmer for 15–20 minutes until thickened.

■ Meanwhile, cook the pasta according to the pack instructions. Drain and toss with the sauce.

Use good-quality sausages with a high meat content, they will give your sauce more body.

Harissa-spiced lamb burgers with sweet potato wedges

30 minutes ■ Serves 4

sweet potatoes 4, cut into long wedges

olive oil

lean minced lamb 400g

red onion 1 small, grated

harissa 1 tbsp

cucumber ½, cut into small dice

natural yoghurt 150ml pot

crusty rolls 4

rocket a small bag, to serve

■ Heat the oven to 200C/fan 180C/gas 6. Toss the sweet potato wedges with 1 tbsp olive oil and some salt. Put on a baking sheet in the oven and cook for about 20 minutes until tender.

■ Mix together the lamb, onion and harissa and season really well. Form into 4 burgers. Griddle or grill for 4–5 minutes on each side until cooked through. Mix the cucumber into the yoghurt and season.

■ Put the burgers into the buns on top of some rocket leaves. Put a dollop of the yoghurt on each burger and serve the rest on the side with the sweet potato wedges.

You can also make small meatballs from this mix and serve in pitta bread with the yoghurt.

Mac 'n' cheese with bacon

45 minutes ■ Serves 2

breadcrumbs 1 handful, fresh and chunky
olive oil
butter 1 tbsp
garlic 1 clove, finely chopped
mustard powder 1 tsp
flour 1 tbsp
whole milk 250ml
Red Leicester 100g, grated
rigatoni or other short pasta 175g
streaky bacon 4 slices, grilled until crisp
and chopped

■ Heat the oven to 200C/fan 180C/gas 6. Put the breadcrumbs on a baking sheet, then drizzle with oil, season and bake for 5 minutes.

■ Melt the butter in a pan. Add the garlic and mustard and cook for 1 minute. Add the flour and whisk on a low heat for 1 minute. Gradually whisk in the milk, then bring to a boil, whisking. Reduce the heat and simmer until thick (about 4 minutes). Stir in the cheese until melted.

■ Boil the pasta until al dente, drain and mix with the cheese sauce and bacon. Spoon into 2 large ramekins. Top each with breadcrumbs and bake for 20 minutes until golden.

To make a veggie version of this, leave out the bacon and top with slices of tomato before sprinkling over the breadcrumbs.

Chorizo with black beans and avocado salsa

1 hour + overnight soaking ■ Serves 4

black turtle beans 250g, soaked overnight in cold water and drained

onion 1, finely chopped

chicken stock 1 litre

chorizo slices 75g, finely sliced

avocado ½, cut into cubes

lime 1

coriander a roughly chopped bunch

soured cream 142ml carton

■ Cook the turtle beans and onion in the chicken stock in a covered pan for 45 minutes or until tender. Stir in half the chorizo then divide between 4 bowls.

■ Mix the avocado with the lime and coriander to make a salsa, then spoon over the beans with the soured cream and remaining chorizo.

Always check the date on dried beans – they have a shelf life and will get tougher the older they are.

Lemon and pepper steak with warm potato salad

30 minutes ■ Serves 2

lemon 1, juiced

olive oil

lean sirloin steaks 2

small salad potatoes 250g

green beans 100g

cherry tomatoes 250g

flat-leaf parsley a small bunch, chopped

■ Mix the lemon juice with 3 tbsp olive oil and a pinch of salt. Take 1 tbsp of this mix and rub over the steaks, then give each a good grinding of black pepper.

■ Boil the potatoes until tender, adding the beans for the last 2–3 minutes. Drain and toss with the tomatoes, parsley and remaining lemon juice mixture.

■ Chargrill or grill the steaks for 2½ minutes each side for medium–rare and serve with the potato salad.

Make sure your steaks are at room temperature before cooking, this will ensure they cook more evenly.

Beef and broccoli stir-fry

20 minutes ∎ Serves 2

broccoli 200g, separated into florets
sunflower oil
sirloin steak 200g, all fat removed
and sliced
garlic 1 clove, sliced
root ginger a thumb-sized piece, shredded
red chillies 2, shredded
spring onions 4, shredded
soy sauce 2 tbsp
sesame oil

∎ Blanch the broccoli in boiling water for a minute and drain.

∎ Heat 1 tbsp sunflower oil in a pan or wok and stir-fry the beef for a couple of minutes. Scoop out, then add the garlic, ginger, chillies and onions and cook for 3–4 minutes. Return the beef with the broccoli, soy and 1 tsp sesame oil. Cook for 2 minutes then serve.

Make sure your broccoli florets are all a similar sizes as this will help them cook more evenly.

Pork, chilli and bean stew

30 minutes ■ Serves 4

olive oil

diced pork 400g

red onion 1, halved and sliced

garlic 2 cloves, sliced

chilli flakes a large pinch

ground cumin 1 tsp

red pepper 1, cut into chunks

chopped tomatoes 400g tin

chicken stock 400ml

small salad potatoes 250g, halved

green beans 100g

coriander ½ a bunch, chopped

■ Heat 1 tbsp olive oil in a large non-stick pan. Season the pork then quickly brown all over. Scoop out then add the onion and garlic and cook for a minute. Add the chilli flakes, cumin and pepper and cook for 2 more minutes.

■ Add back the pork with the tinned tomatoes and chicken stock. Bring to a simmer and add the potatoes. Cook for 10–15 minutes then add the beans and cook for another 5 minutes. Season and scatter over the coriander to finish.

You can use kidney beans rather than green beans for a more storecupboard version of this stew.

Poached salmon with green herb and mustard sauce

20 minutes ■ Serves 2

skinless salmon fillets 2

tarragon chopped, 2 tbsp

flat-leaf parsley 2 tbsp, chopped

Dijon mustard 2 tsp

white wine vinegar 2 tbsp

olive oil 2 tbsp

new potatoes and watercress to serve

■ Bring a shallow pan of water to a simmer. Drop in the salmon, put a lid on the pan and cook for 5–6 minutes.

■ Put all the other ingredients in a small food processor and whizz until smooth (if it's too thick, add a splash of water).

■ Lift the salmon up and drain. Serve the salmon with potatoes, watercress and the sauce.

You can mix and match the herbs in the sauce, try chives, coriander or basil for a different flavour.

Cornish sea bass with frizzled chillies, ginger and spring onions

35 minutes ■ Serves 4

root ginger 3cm piece

spring onions 6

red chillies 2

oil 2 tbsp, for frying

garlic 2 cloves, finely sliced

sea bass fillets 4, about 180g each, skin on (or 8 if the fish are very small)

spiced black rice vinegar 2 tbsp or ordinary rice vinegar 1 tbsp

sesame oil

coriander a handful of leaves, roughly chopped

■ Shred the ginger, spring onions and red chillies finely. Heat the oil in a wok, and when it is very hot, fry the ginger, spring onions and chillies in turn until they frizzle up. They should hiss and spit. Scoop them out the second they're done. Fry the garlic for a few seconds until it is light brown then scoop out.

■ Tip out all but a dribble of oil and add the sea bass skin-side down, 2 fillets at a time for about 4–6 minutes. Press them into the wok so they don't curl up, the skin should crisp and brown quickly and the fillets cook through. Turn them over if you need to. Keep warm while you cook the next batch.

■ Serve the fillets with the frizzled chillies, ginger and spring onions on top, drizzle over the vinegar and sesame oil and sprinkle over the coriander.

Look for spiced black rice vinegar in Asian grocers and online.

Spaghetti with anchovy, chilli and breadcrumbs

15 minutes ■ Serves 2

spaghetti 150g

olive oil

anchovies 4, finely chopped

garlic 1 clove, crushed

red chilli 1, finely chopped

parsley a small bunch, chopped

ciabatta a handful of rough breadcrumbs, tossed in 1 tsp olive oil and toasted until golden in a high oven

■ Cook the spaghetti according to the pack instructions. Drain, reserving 1 tbsp of the cooking water.

■ Heat 4 tbsp olive oil, add the anchovies, garlic and chilli and gently sizzle for a couple of minutes. Toss with the spaghetti, parsley and cooking water. Sprinkle over the breadcrumbs to finish.

Adding a little of the cooking water helps make a sauce for the pasta.

Chilli prawn noodles

30 minutes ■ Serves 2

chicken stock 600ml
ginger 2cm piece, sliced
garlic 2 cloves, bashed
lemon grass a stalk, bashed
soy sauce
vegetables a mix of mangetout,
baby sweetcorn, baby pak choi,
baby carrots 200g
large peeled prawns 100g
flat rice noodles 100g
red chillies shredded, to serve
spring onions shredded, to serve

■ Put the stock in a pan and add the ginger, garlic and lemon grass and simmer gently for 10 minutes, then strain. Add a splash of soy sauce.

■ Gently simmer the veg in the stock for 2–3 minutes. Add the prawns and just heat through. Cook the noodles separately according to the pack instructions until just tender.

■ Divide the cooked noodles between 2 bowls. Pour over the hot soup and veg. Finish with the shredded chillies and spring onions.

There's no need to slice the garlic and lemon grass – just bruise them and they'll release all their flavour into the stock.

Linguine with tuna, lemon and dill

20 minutes ■ Serves 2

linguine 150g

tuna 200g tin, drained and flaked

red onion ½ small, finely sliced

lemon 1, zested and juiced

olive oil 1 tbsp

dill a small bunch, chopped

■ Cook the pasta according to the pack instructions. Mix together the rest of the ingredients in a large bowl and season. Drain the pasta and toss everything together.

Look for tuna packed in good olive oil as this will add more flavour.

Citrus salmon with herb and caper crushed potatoes

30 minutes ■ Serves 2

salmon 2 skinless fillets

lemon 1, juiced

orange 1, juiced

olive oil

new potatoes 300g

Dijon mustard 1 tbsp

basil ½ small bunch, chopped

capers 1 tbsp, rinsed and drained

■ Heat the oven to 180C/fan 160C/gas 4. Put the salmon in a freezer bag with half the lemon juice, all the orange juice and 1 tbsp olive oil, season well and leave for 10 minutes.

■ Tip out the salmon and marinade into a shallow ovenproof dish and bake for 6–8 minutes until just cooked through.

■ Boil the potatoes until tender. Gently crush with 1 tbsp olive oil, the rest of the lemon juice, mustard, basil and capers. Serve with the salmon and any juices from the dish.

Don't leave the salmon in the marinade longer than 20 minutes otherwise the citrus juices will start to 'cook' the fish.

Trout ceviche

25 minutes + marinating ■ Serves 4

trout fillets 4
limes 2, juiced
red chilli 1 small, finely chopped
onion ½, very finely chopped
tomatoes 2, seeded, skinned and finely chopped
avocado ½, peeled and finely chopped
coriander a handful of leaves

■ Slice the trout carefully into strips, cutting into the fish on a diagonal. Lay the strips in a glass or ceramic dish and pour over the lime juice, chilli and onion. Cover and leave in the fridge for an hour. Check all the fish is in contact with the lime and rearrange the strips if you need to, then leave for another hour.

■ Arrange the fish on plates to serve, season with a little salt and scatter the tomato, avocado and coriander over.

Trout has a more subtle flavour than salmon so is ideal for a light summer lunch. Look for organic or sustainably produced trout.

Smoked haddock with chive, pea and potato crush

20 minutes ■ Serves 2

small salad potatoes 300g, halved
frozen peas 2 handfuls
butter 50g
smoked haddock fillets 2, about 150g each
white wine or **chicken stock** a splash
chives ½ a small bunch, chopped

■ Cook the potatoes until tender, then add the frozen peas for the last 2 minutes of cooking. Gently crush with half the butter.

■ Heat the rest of the butter in a pan and cook the haddock for 3 minutes on each side.

■ Remove the haddock then add a splash of wine or chicken stock and reduce a little. Stir in the chives.

■ Put the potato on 2 plates, top with the haddock and the chive butter.

Look for naturally dyed haddock rather than the bright yellow stuff.

Cod with tomato and chorizo sauce

20 minutes ■ Serves 2

....

olive oil

garlic 1 clove, sliced

chorizo 4 thin slices from the deli counter, cut into matchsticks

dried chilli flakes a pinch

chopped tomatoes 400g tin

cod or other sustainable white fish, 2 thick skinless fillets

green beans cooked to serve

■ Heat 1 tbsp olive oil in a pan then cook the garlic and chorizo for a few minutes. Add the chilli and tomatoes and simmer for 10 minutes until thickened, season.

■ Meanwhile, rub the fish with a little more oil, season and grill or steam until cooked through, about 4–6 minutes. Serve the fish with the sauce and green beans.

You can also serve this sauce with roast chicken pieces or just tossed through cooked pasta.

Prawn orecchiette with basil butter

15 minutes ■ Serves 2

orecchiette 150g

butter 50g

garlic 1 clove, crushed

peeled raw king prawns 150g

basil a handful of leaves, shredded

lemon a squeeze of juice

■ Cook the orecchiette according to the pack instructions.

■ Melt the butter in a pan and sizzle the garlic for a couple of minutes. Tip in the prawns and cook until pink.

■ Drain the pasta well and toss it with the prawn butter, basil and a squeeze of lemon.

Orecchiette is small 'ear'-shaped pasta, which holds the butter really well. Something like fusilli would also work for this.

Salmon sashimi plate

10 minutes ■ Serves 2

skinless salmon fillet 300g

root ginger 3cm piece, peeled and cut into matchsticks

chives 2 tbsp, chopped

sesame seeds 1 tsp

soy sauce 1 tbsp

sesame oil 2 tsp

■ Slice the salmon as thinly as possible and lay over 2 plates. Scatter over the ginger, chives and sesame seeds.

■ Mix the soy sauce and sesame oil and drizzle over before serving.

You'll need the freshest fish you can get for this – buy your salmon from the fishmonger and tell him you are eating it raw.

Herb and pea fishcakes

45 minutes ■ Serves 4

cod or other skinless white sustainable fish
fillets, 300g

spring onions 4, finely shredded

milk 3 tbsp

butter 50g

potatoes 500g, peeled and cut into chunks

lemon ½, plus wedges to serve

frozen peas 150g, defrosted **dill** a handful,
finely chopped

parsley a handful, chopped

flour 1 tbsp for dusting

salad to serve

■ Steam the fish, then cool and flake. Put the
spring onions in a pan with the milk and half
the butter and cook until softened.

■ Boil the potatoes until tender, cool a little,
then roughly mash with the spring onion
mixture. Season, adding a squeeze of lemon.
Add the peas, fish and herbs. Mix, keeping
the fish in big flakes.

■ Form into 8 fishcakes. Dust lightly with
flour. Heat the remaining butter in a non-stick
pan and cook the cakes for 3–4 minutes each
side until golden. Serve with lemon wedges
and salad.

**Adding peas to the mix gives a juicier
texture to the finished fishcakes.**

Prawn noodles with peanut dressing

20 minutes ■ Serves 2

peanut butter 2 tbsp

sesame oil 1 tsp

soy sauce 1 tbsp

chilli sauce 1 tbsp

egg noodles 100g

cooked peeled prawns 150g

mangetout 50g, halved lengthways

red chilli 1, sliced

spring onions 2, shredded

■ Whisk the peanut butter, sesame oil, soy and chilli sauce with 2 tbsp boiling water to make a dressing.

■ Cook the noodles according to the pack instructions. Drain, then put in a bowl with the prawns, mangetout and dressing. Toss together and serve sprinkled with chilli and spring onions.

Use whatever peanut butter you have for this – a crunchy one will give more texture to the dish.

Tandoori salmon with spicy mango and cucumber chutney

20 minutes + chilling ■ Serves 4

Greek yoghurt 100g, plus extra to serve

garlic 2 cloves, crushed

tandoori or other Indian curry paste 1 tbsp

lemon 1, juiced

root ginger 1 tsp, grated

chilli powder 1½ tsp

salmon fillet 500g, skin on

basmati rice, to serve

coriander leaves, to serve

CHUTNEY

mango ½, peeled and finely chopped

cucumber ½ small, finely chopped

red onion ½, finely chopped

green chilli 1 medium, deseeded and finely chopped

mint 1 tbsp, chopped

■ Mix the yoghurt, garlic, tandoori or other curry paste, half the lemon juice, the ginger and 1 tsp of the chilli powder together in a small bowl and season. Spread over the salmon and chill until using (at least 20 minutes).

■ Mix the chutney ingredients together. Add the remaining lemon juice and chilli powder, season and set aside.

■ Grill the salmon until blackened at the edges, about 6–8 minutes depending on the thickness of the fish. Serve with basmati rice, yoghurt, coriander and the fresh chutney.

The marinade and fresh chutney could also be used with chicken or lamb chops.

Spiced couscous with chicken and almonds

20 minutes ■ Serves 2

Indian curry paste 2 tsp

apricots 6 ready-to-eat, chopped

chicken stock 150ml, hot

couscous 150g

cooked chicken breast 1 large skinless, shredded

spring onions 2, sliced (use the green parts as well)

blanched almonds 2 tbsp, toasted

flat-leaf parsley a small bunch, chopped

natural yoghurt 150ml

■ Mix the curry paste and apricots with the chicken stock until the paste has dissolved. Then put the couscous in a bowl and pour over the stock. Cover with clingfilm and leave for 5 minutes.

■ Break up the couscous with a fork and stir through the chicken, spring onions, almonds and half the parsley. Mix the rest of the yoghurt with the parsley. Serve the couscous with the yoghurt drizzled over.

Look for a curry paste that doesn't need cooking first for this recipe, otherwise you'll need to fry it for 3–4 minutes before adding to the stock.

Chicken baked with globe artichokes and lemon

1 hour 40 minutes ■ Serves 4

onion 1, cut into wedges

garlic 3 cloves, squashed

lemon 1, cut into eighths

white wine 250ml

chicken 1, about 2kg

globe artichokes 4, cleaned, quartered, chokes scraped out

olive oil

parsley 1 bunch, roughly chopped

■ Heat the oven to 190C/fan 170/gas 5. Put the onion, garlic, lemon and white wine in the bottom of a large casserole and put the chicken on top. Season well. Add the artichokes around the edge and drizzle with oil. Cook for 1 hour 20 minutes or until the chicken is cooked through (check by piercing the thigh, the juices should run clear. If not, keep cooking until they do).

■ Lift the chicken out of the pan and rest for 15 minutes, keep the veg warm. Stir the parsley through the vegetables in the pan and serve with the chicken.

If you want to prep the artichokes ahead, rub them all over with lemon juice to stop them discolouring.

Smoky paprika chicken with lemon and olives

20 minutes ■ Serves 2

chicken breasts 2

smoked paprika 2 tsp

olive oil 1 tbsp

lemon 1, zest cut into strips

red onion ½ small, sliced

pitted black olives 10

flat-leaf parsley 2 tbsp, chopped

■ Rub the chicken with the smoked paprika and olive oil. Chargill or grill for 4–5 minutes per side until cooked through. Slice, then toss with the lemon zest and red onion, black olives and parsley.

Smoked paprika comes in hot and sweet versions — either would work for this.

Vietnamese coleslaw with grilled chicken

35 minutes ■ Serves 4

Chinese cabbage ½ head
summer cabbage ¾ head
celery 2 sticks
carrot 1, medium
mint and **coriander leaves** 1 handful
of each
chicken thighs 8
limes 2, cut into wedges
DRESSING
rice vinegar 6 tbsp
caster sugar 2 tsp
fish sauce 3 tsp
chilli 1, finely sliced

■ Slice the cabbages, celery and carrot finely on a mandolin, chop the mint and coriander and toss them all together.

■ Make the dressing by whisking all the ingredients together. Brush the chicken with a little dressing and grill until cooked.

■ Dress the coleslaw. Serve with the chicken and lime.

Any leftover coleslaw will keep for a couple of days in the fridge.

Lime leaf chicken with sweet chilli and peanut dipping sauce

30 minutes + chilling ■ Serves 4

lime leaves 35

garlic 2 cloves

fish sauce 2 tsp

honey 2 tsp

spring onions 3, chopped

vegetable oil

chicken breasts 4, cut into small cubes

PEANUT CHILLI SAUCE

rice vinegar 150ml

caster sugar 175g

coriander 1 tbsp, chopped

red chilli 1 medium, finely sliced

roasted peanuts 1 tbsp, ground

■ Soak 20 wooden skewers in water. Take 15 lime leaves, pull off the stalks and finely chop. Leave the remaining ones whole. Combine the garlic, fish sauce, honey, spring onions and vegetable oil in the food processor.

■ Skewer the chicken along with 1 whole lime leaf, put in a flat dish and pour over the marinade. Chill for at least 30 minutes or until ready to grill.

■ Make the chilli sauce by heating the rice vinegar and sugar. After it boils, turn the heat down and cook for about 3 minutes until thickened. Cool, then add the remaining ingredients. Cook the chicken on a barbecue, grill pan or frying pan until brown, about 2–3 minutes each side. Serve with the chilli dipping sauce.

Lime leaves give a citrus flavour to marinades, curries and soups that is intensely fragrant. Find them in Asian shops and freeze any left over. If you can't get hold of them, substitute 2 tbsp lime zest.

Chicken breasts with grape and pecan stuffing

45 minutes ■ Serves 6

chicken supremes or **breast fillets** skin on, 6

onion 1 small, finely chopped

butter

fresh breadcrumbs 2 tbsp

seedless red grapes 18, quartered

pecans 12, roughly chopped

orange 2, 1 zested and juiced, 1 cut into wedges, to serve

tarragon 2 tbsp, chopped

■ Heat the oven to 180C/fan 160C/gas 4. Make a sideways cut into each supreme or breast so you can fold the top half back like a book. Bat each side out slightly with a rolling pin to make the meat a bit thinner.

■ Fry the onion in a little butter until soft then stir in the breadcrumbs, grapes, pecans, orange zest and tarragon (reserve some tarragon to garnish later) and season.

■ Divide the stuffing between the chicken breasts and fold the skin side of the chicken back over the filling. Smear a little butter over the skin and move carefully to a shallow roasting tin. Roast for 15 minutes or until the chicken is cooked through and the skin crisp and golden.

■ Drizzle with orange juice and serve sprinkled with the reserved tarragon, the juices from the tin and orange wedges.

Make sure you cook the breasts in a shallow tin – a deep tin will just steam rather than roast them.

Coconut chicken noodles

30 minutes ■ Serves 4

rice noodles 100g

vegetable oil

boneless skinless chicken thighs 500g

Thai red curry paste 4 tbsp

soft brown sugar 2 tbsp

tamarind purée 100g

fish sauce 2 tbsp

limes 2, zested and juiced

coconut milk 2 x 400ml tins

fine green beans 250g, trimmed and cut into pieces

button mushrooms 100g, halved

coriander leaves, to serve

■ Soak the rice noodles in boiling water until al dente. Drain, rinse in cold water and drain again. Drizzle with a bit of oil and set aside.

■ Slice the chicken into small pieces and brown in a medium pan with 1 tsp vegetable oil. Season, and when the chicken is tender (about 8 minutes), add the curry paste. Fry for 3 minutes then add the sugar, tamarind, fish sauce, lime zest and juice, and coconut milk. Simmer gently for 10 minutes then add the beans and mushrooms in the last 3 minutes.

■ Divide the noodles between 4 large bowls. Make sure the curry is near boiling, then pour over the noodles. Serve in large bowls sprinkled with coriander.

Thai red curry paste and tamarind purée can be found in the Asian or spice section at most supermarkets.

Yakitori chicken skewers with miso

20 minutes ■ Serves 2

miso paste 4 tbsp

sugar 2 tbsp

mirin 4 tbsp

chicken thigh fillets 250g, cut into
2cm chunks

spring onions 3 fat ones, cut into
2cm chunks

■ Mix the miso, sugar and mirin until the sugar dissolves. Thread the chicken and onions alternately onto skewers. If using wooden skewers, soak in cold water for 15 minutes.

■ Brush the skewers with some of the sauce, then grill until cooked through, brushing with more sauce as you go.

Find miso and mirin in healthfood shops and the Asian sections of supermarkets.

Chicken with salsa verde

30 minutes ■ Serves 2

lemon 1, juiced

parsley ½ a small bunch

basil ½ a small bunch

capers 1 tbsp, rinsed and drained

garlic ½ clove

Dijon mustard 1 tsp

olive oil

chicken breasts 2, skinless

cannellini beans 400g tin

rocket 50g

■ To make the salsa, whizz the lemon juice, herbs, capers, garlic, mustard and 2 tbsp oil in a food processor (add a little water if needed).

■ Chargrill or grill the chicken on both sides until cooked. Heat the beans, drain, then toss with the rocket and half the salsa. Slice the chicken and dress with the rest of the salsa.

This would also work with butter beans or chickpeas, in place of the cannellini beans.

Griddled courgette, chicken and lentils with mint yoghurt

25 minutes ■ Serves 2

Puy lentils 100g

chicken stock 1 cube

chicken thighs 4, sliced into ribbons

olive oil

garam masala ½ tsp

courgettes 2, sliced into strips

garlic 1 clove, crushed

coriander ½ small bunch, chopped

lemon ½, juiced

natural yoghurt 5 tbsp

mint sauce 1 tsp

■ Simmer the lentils with the stock cube, in enough water to cover, until tender, then drain. Meanwhile, heat a griddle (chargrill) to high.

■ Toss the chicken with 1 tsp olive oil, then the garam masala. Toss the courgette strips with 1 tsp olive oil and the garlic and season. Griddle the chicken and courgettes on both sides.

■ Toss the lentils, chicken, courgettes, coriander and lemon juice together. Mix the yoghurt with the mint sauce and drizzle over.

Make sure your griddle is really hot and oil the food rather than the pan to stop it sticking.

Jerk-spiced chicken with coconut rice

25 minutes ■ Serves 2

skinless chicken thigh fillets 6, cut
into chunks
red pepper 1, cut into chunks
Jamaican jerk paste 1 tbsp
basmati rice 100g
half-fat coconut milk 180ml tin
frozen peas a handful, defrosted
coriander a small bunch, chopped
spring onions 2, finely chopped

■ Soak 4 skewers in water for 15 minutes.

■ Toss the chicken and pepper in the jerk
paste and leave to marinate for 10 minutes.

■ Put the rice, coconut milk and 75ml water
in a pan and season. Bring to a simmer then
put on a lid and cook gently until all the liquid
has been absorbed and the rice is cooked,
adding the peas for the last 3 minutes of
cooking. Stir through half the coriander
and the spring onions.

■ Thread the chicken and peppers onto the
4 skewers. Grill for 8–10 minutes, turning
until cooked through. Serve with the coconut
rice, then sprinkle over a little coriander.

If you don't have any skewers, just grill the
thighs whole and serve with the rice.

Yoghurt-spiced chicken with almond and coriander rice

30 minutes ■ Serves 2

natural yoghurt 150ml

madras or other Indian curry paste 1 tbsp

chicken breasts 2

butter

onion 1, halved and sliced

cardamom pods 3, squashed

brown basmati rice 150g

chicken stock 350ml

flaked almonds 1 tbsp, toasted

red chilli 1, finely chopped (optional)

coriander ½ a bunch, chopped

■ Mix the yoghurt and curry paste and toss with the chicken breasts. Heat a knob of butter in a wide shallow pan with a lid.

■ Cook the onion and cardamom for 5 minutes then tip in the rice and stock. Bring to a simmer, cover and cook until all the stock is absorbed and the rice is tender (you might need to add a little more stock).

■ Griddle or grill the chicken breasts until golden and cooked through. Stir the almonds, chilli, if using, and coriander through the rice. Slice the breasts and sit on top of the rice.

It's always best to toast nuts in a dry pan before using as it really brings out their flavour.

Light chicken Caesar

20 minutes ■ Serves 2

ciabatta 2 slices, cut into chunks

olive oil

sea salt flakes

half-fat crème fraîche 4 tbsp

Dijon mustard 1 tsp

Worcestershire sauce ½ tsp

garlic ½ clove, crushed

parmesan 30g, finely grated plus a few shavings

lemon ½, juiced

little gem lettuce 2, leaves separated and torn if large

cooked skinless chicken breast 1, sliced

spring onions 2, shredded

■ Heat the oven to 200C/fan 180C/gas 6. Toss the bread with 1 tbsp olive oil and some salt flakes. Bake for 10–15 minutes until golden.

■ Mix the crème fraîche, Dijon mustard, Worcestershire sauce, garlic and parmesan with a squeeze of lemon juice and a splash of water. Season.

■ Toss the lettuce with half the dressing and divide between 2 plates. Top with chicken, croutons and spring onions. Drizzle over the rest of the dressing. Shave over a little parmesan to finish.

If you like anchovies in your Caesar salad you could add a few whole marinated ones to the finished dish.

Chicken hotpot

45 minutes ■ Serves 2

butter
leek 1, halved lengthways and sliced
garlic 1 clove, crushed
new potatoes 250g, halved or quartered
boneless skinless chicken thigh fillets 4, all fat removed and cut into chunks
white wine a glass
chicken stock 300ml
tarragon leaves from a small bunch
half-fat crème fraîche 2 tbsp
green beans 100g, blanched (optional)
crusty brown bread (optional)

■ Heat a knob of butter in a shallow pan. Add the leek and garlic and cook until softened.

■ Add the new potatoes, chicken, wine and chicken stock, cover and simmer for about 30 minutes until the potatoes and chicken are cooked. Season and stir in the tarragon and crème fraîche. Serve with green beans and crusty bread, if you like.

Chicken thighs are cheaper than breasts, and are brilliant in casseroles as they don't dry out.

Asparagus with tarragon salsa verde

10 minutes ■ Serves 4

asparagus 2 bundles, trimmed
lemon 1, juiced
tarragon 1 large bunch
parsley 2 tbsp, chopped
capers 1 tbsp, drained and rinsed
balsamic vinegar 1 tbsp
olive oil
sourdough to serve

■ Cook the asparagus in salted, simmering water in a deep frying pan until tender – how long this takes will depend on how thick the spears are. They should be tender enough to just bend under their own weight when held at one end.

■ Meanwhile, whizz the remaining ingredients except the oil and bread – you can make the mixture chunky or fine. Add enough oil to make a thick but spoonable dressing and season. Serve with toasted sourdough.

The British asparagus season lasts eight short weeks, so make the most of it. Visit british-asparagus.co.uk.

Marinated radishes with pomegranate molasses

10 minutes ■ Serves 2

radishes 1 large bunch
orange 1, juiced
honey 1 tsp
chilli oil a dash
pumpkin seeds 3 tbsp
pomegranate molasses
mint a handful of small leaves

■ Slice the radishes as finely as possible (use a mandolin if you have one, but be careful). Tip them into a bowl with the orange juice, honey and chilli oil and toss. Tip onto a plate and spread out in a single layer.

■ Dry-fry the pumpkin seeds in a frying pan until just browned, scatter them over the radishes, then drizzle on a little pomegranate molasses and sprinkle over the mint leaves.

Pomegranate molasses is a sweet and sour syrup used widely in Middle Eastern cooking. Find it in delis and large supermarkets.

Herbed cream cheese with cucumber salad

15 minutes + chilling ■ Serves 4

fromage blanc or **soft mild goat's cheese**
300g

chives, **flat-leaf parsley** and **tarragon** all
chopped, 3 tbsp

shallot 1, finely chopped

garlic 1 clove, crushed

red wine vinegar 1 tsp

crusty bread, to serve

CUCUMBER SALAD

cucumber ½

chives and **tarragon**, 2 tbsp, chopped

lemon ½, juiced

olive oil for dressing

■ Beat the cheese, herbs, shallot, garlic and red wine vinegar together and season well. Spoon into ramekins or moulds lined with cheesecloth and chill overnight.

■ For the cucumber salad, take strips off the skin of the cucumber with a peeler, then cut it into fine slices, put in a bowl with the salad herbs and lemon juice and season.

■ Arrange some cucumber on 4 plates, drizzle with oil and serve with the cream cheese and bread.

Cucumbers are at their crunchiest and juiciest in summer and their crisp texture is a good foil for soft cheese.

Halloumi salad with houmous dressing and pitta crisps

20 minutes ■ Serves 2

wholemeal pitta bread 2

tomatoes 2, cut into chunks

red onion ½, sliced

cucumber ½, cut into chunks

olive oil

lemon ½, juiced

halloumi 250g, cut into chunks

dried oregano

houmous 2 tbsp

natural yoghurt 75ml

■ Heat the oven to 180C/fan 160C/gas 4. To make the pitta crisps, separate the pittas into 2 halves, cut into triangles and bake for 5–10 minutes until crisp.

■ Toss the tomatoes, onion, and cucumber with 1 tbsp olive oil and the lemon juice.

■ Sprinkle the halloumi with a little oregano then grill or fry until golden. Mix the houmous and yoghurt with a little water to make a dressing and season. Toss the halloumi with the salad, drizzle over the houmous dressing and serve with the pitta crisps.

You can serve these pitta crisps with paté or dips as well.

Courgette pissaladière

1 hour 30 minutes ■ Serves 4

plain flour 250g
easy-blend dried yeast 1½ tsp
sugar a pinch
egg 1, beaten
olive oil
garlic 3 cloves, crushed
Spanish onion 1, finely sliced
courgettes 500g, sliced
parmesan a block for making curls

■ Put the flour in a mixing bowl with the yeast and a pinch each of salt and sugar. Make a well in the centre and add the egg, 1 tbsp olive oil and 75ml lukewarm water. Mix until the dough comes together, adding a little more water if needed. Turn out onto a lightly floured worksurface and knead until smooth. Lightly oil a large non-stick baking sheet, then roll the dough out on top into a 40 x 30cm rectangle.

■ Fry the garlic in a little olive oil and brush the mixture over the dough. Fry the onion in a little olive oil and spread this over the dough. Lay the courgette slices in overlapping lines over the dough and drizzle with a little more oil. Season well. Cover loosely with clingfilm and leave to rise for about 20–25 minutes.

■ Heat the oven to 190C/fan 170C/gas 5. Bake for about 20–25 minutes. Cover with curls of parmesan, cut into squares and serve warm.

Pissaladière is a variety of pizza made in southern France. Use a mix of yellow and green courgettes together, if you like.

Cauliflower fritters with lemon and capers

30 minutes ■ Serves 4

cauliflower 1, broken into florets
plain flour 100g, plus a little for dusting
eggs 2, separated
fizzy water 175ml
oil for deep frying
lemons 2, 1 juiced and 1 cut into wedges
baby capers 1 tbsp, rinsed and drained
parsley 2 tbsp, finely chopped

■ Steam the cauliflower for 4 minutes or until just tender, then cool. Put the flour in large bowl and whisk in the egg yolks plus a pinch of salt followed by the fizzy water. Whisk the egg whites to soft peaks and fold them in.

■ Heat a deep-fat fryer or wok filled one-third full with oil to 190C (a piece of bread dropped into the oil will immediately rise to the surface and fizz). Keep an eye on it, though, to make sure it doesn't get too hot). Dust the cauliflower in a little flour to help the batter stick, then coat it thoroughly in the batter. Lower in batches into the oil and cook for 2–3 minutes or until golden and crisp.

■ Sprinkle the cauliflower with a little salt while still hot and put on a plate. Mix the lemon juice with the capers and parsley and spoon a little over each floret. Serve with lemon wedges.

Look for cauliflowers with a dense creamy head and no discolouration.

Courgette, tomato and gruyère gratin

1 hour ■ Serves 2

garlic 1 clove

olive oil

plum tomatoes 400g tin, drained

basil leaves a handful

tomatoes 3, sliced

courgettes 2, sliced

gruyère 100g, grated

crusty bread, to serve

■ Heat the oven to 200C/fan 180C/gas 6. Sizzle the garlic in 2 tbsp olive oil for 2 minutes then tip in the tomatoes. Simmer for 10 minutes until thickened then stir in the basil and season.

■ Divide the sauce between 2 shallow gratin dishes. Arrange overlapping rows of tomato and courgette, sprinkling some gruyère between them. Drizzle with oil, season and bake covered with foil for 20 minutes. Remove the foil and bake for another 15–20 minutes. Serve with crusty bread.

Make sure the tomato sauce has enough time to thicken as water will come out of the courgettes when cooking.

Beetroot, dill and feta frittata

10 minutes ■ Serves 2

onion 1, thinly sliced
olive oil
cooked beetroot 2, sliced
feta 100g, crumbled
dill small handful, chopped
eggs 4, beaten with seasoning

■ Cook the onion in 2 tbsp oil in a small frying pan until golden. Layer the beetroot, feta and dill over, then pour the eggs in. Cook on a medium–high heat until nearly firm. Put under the grill for 3–4 minutes until the top is set.

Use a small, deep frying pan for this to get a better depth to your frittata.

Field mushrooms, spinach and goat's cheese on toast

20 minutes ■ Serves 2

field mushrooms or other large flat
mushrooms 4

olive oil

garlic 2 cloves, sliced

spring onions 2, sliced

spinach 100g, washed

goat's cheese 100g log, sliced

ciabatta 4 slices, toasted

■ Heat the grill to high. Brush the mushrooms with olive oil, season and grill until tender. Cook the garlic and spring onions in olive oil until soft then stir in the spinach until wilted. Fill the mushrooms with the spinach mix, top with goat's cheese and grill until golden. Serve on top of toasted ciabatta.

Mushrooms grilled in this way also make a great filling for a meatless burger.

Ricotta and spinach filo parcels

1 hour ■ Makes 12

ricotta 250g tub

lemon 1, zested

parmesan 3 tbsp, grated

onion 1 large, sliced

butter

garlic 1 clove, crushed

young spinach 300g, chopped

filo pastry 6 large sheets, unrolled and cut into rectangles

■ Heat the oven to 200C/fan 180C/gas 6. Mix the ricotta, lemon and parmesan. Cook the onion in a knob of butter with the garlic until soft.

■ Add the spinach to the onion and cook until wilted. Cool, stir into the ricotta mix and season. Melt a little butter and brush over a pastry rectangle, cover with another and brush again.

■ Put 1 tbsp of filling in a corner, fold into a triangle then fold twice more. Brush again. Repeat to make 12. Bake for 15–20 minutes. Serve with salad.

Keep filo pastry covered with a damp tea towel as you work to stop it drying out.

Baked tomatoes with oregano and pecorino

1 hour ■ Serves 2

tomatoes 500g, a mixture of varieties

oregano 4 sprigs

garlic 2 cloves, thinly sliced

olive oil

pecorino cheese 40g, grated

toasted bread, to serve

■ Heat the oven to 200C/fan 180C/gas 6.
■ Cut a waist around each tomato with a sharp knife and pack the tomatoes into a shallow baking dish. Pull the leaves off the oregano and sprinkle them over and around the tomatoes, along with the garlic. Pour over a good slug of olive oil and season well. Bake for 35 minutes then sprinkle on the cheese and return to the oven for 10 minutes. Serve with toasted bread.

Tomatoes are at their best at the end of summer in August and September when they've had a good dose of sun. Use different shapes and sizes for this dish to make it look interesting.

Baked new potatoes with Camembert and poppy seeds

40 minutes ■ Serves 4

new potatoes 500g, washed and halved

Camembert 250g, thickly sliced

orange 1, zested and juiced

poppy seeds 1 tbsp

olive oil

■ Heat the oven to 180C/fan 160C/gas 4.

■ Tip the potatoes into a shallow baking dish, arrange the Camembert on top and then sprinkle over the orange zest and juice followed by the poppy seeds. Season well and add a few drops of olive oil.

■ Bake for 30 minutes or until the potatoes are cooked through.

May is the height of the Jersey Royal potato season – their rich, buttery flavour is perfect for this recipe.

Soft polenta with roast butternut squash and blue cheese

30 minutes ■ Serves 2

butternut squash 500g, diced
olive oil
instant polenta 100g
butter 50g
parmesan 2 tbsp, grated
gorgonzola 75g, crumbled

■ Heat the oven to 200C/fan 180C/gas 6. Toss the squash with 1 tbsp olive oil and some seasoning then roast for 20 minutes or until tender.

■ Make up the polenta following the pack instructions – it should be soft enough to spoon. Season well, then beat in the butter and parmesan. Serve the polenta topped with the squash and gorgonzola.

Use instant polenta for this – it takes minutes to make and is much easier to handle than the regular variety.

Penne with gorgonzola, walnuts and spinach

15 minutes ■ Serves 2

penne 150g

spinach 100g, roughly chopped

gorgonzola 100g, crumbled

single cream 4 tbsp

walnut halves a handful, toasted and roughly chopped

■ Cook the penne according to the pack instructions. Put the spinach in a colander and pour the pasta and cooking water over to wilt the spinach. Leave to drain.

■ Mix the cheese, cream and walnuts with salt and lots of pepper then stir through the hot pasta and spinach.

Gorgonzola is a really creamy blue cheese, but Dolcelatte or Roquefort would also work well.

Porcini and spinach risotto

30 minutes ■ Serves 2

dried porcini 25g
butter 50g
onion 1 small, finely chopped
garlic 1 clove, crushed
chestnut mushrooms 200g, sliced
risotto rice 150g
white wine a glass
vegetable stock 750ml, kept simmering
spinach 100g, washed and chopped
parmesan few shavings (optional)

■ Soak the porcini in a cup of boiling water for 10 minutes. Strain the liquid through a sieve to remove any grit and keep for the risotto. Roughly chop the porcini.

■ Heat the butter in a wide shallow pan and cook the onion and garlic until softened. Add the chestnut mushrooms and cook for 5 minutes, then add the porcini and risotto rice and stir until coated.

■ Tip in the wine and bubble until it's all absorbed. Gradually add the stock and porcini soaking liquid, stirring until the rice is tender but still has a little bite (you might not need all the stock). Stir through the spinach until just wilted. Serve sprinkled with a little parmesan, if you like.

Dried porcini are a great way to increase flavour in recipes without spending a fortune on wild mushrooms.

Linguine with fresh puttanesca sauce

15 minutes ■ Serves 2

linguine 150g

cherry tomatoes 250g, chopped

capers 2 tbsp, rinsed

garlic ½ clove, crushed

flat-leaf parsley a small bunch, chopped

red chilli 1, finely chopped

green olives 12, pitted and chopped

lemon 1, juiced

olive oil

■ Cook the linguine according to the pack instructions. Put the rest of the ingredients into a large bowl, add 3 tbsp olive oil, season and toss together. Drain the pasta and toss with the sauce.

You could also use this sauce as a topping for bruschetta.

Artichoke, lemon and parmesan pasta

15 minutes ■ Serves 2

spaghetti 150g

marinated artichoke hearts 100g, drained and sliced

lemon 1, juiced and zested

parmesan 25g, finely grated

basil ½ a small bunch, shredded

olive oil

■ Cook the spaghetti according to the pack instructions. Put the rest of the ingredients in a large bowl with 1 tbsp olive oil, then season really well and mix. Drain the pasta, keep 2 tbsp of the cooking water, then toss everything together.

You can buy cooked, marinated artichoke hearts in jars or from the deli counter of most supermarkets.

Rigatoni with courgette, lemon and parmesan

20 minutes ■ Serves 2

rigatoni 150g
olive oil
garlic 1 clove, crushed
red chilli 1, finely chopped (optional)
courgettes 2, grated
lemon 1, zested and juiced
parmesan 30g, grated

■ Cook the pasta according to the pack instructions. Drain, keeping back 2 tbsp of the cooking liquid. Heat 2 tbsp olive oil in a frying pan and add the garlic and chilli, if using, and cook for a minute.

■ Add the courgettes and then fry for 5–6 minutes until softened. Stir through the lemon zest and juice. Toss the pasta with the courgettes, parmesan and pasta cooking liquid and serve.

You can leave the chilli out of this if you don't want so much heat.

Leek and parmesan risotto

30 minutes ■ Serves 2

vegetable or **chicken stock** 750ml

butter 25g

olive oil 1 tbsp

spring onions 4, chopped

leeks 2, trimmed and finely chopped

garlic 2 cloves, sliced

arborio rice 150g

white wine a glass

parmesan 25g, finely grated

■ Bring the stock to a simmer. Heat a large wide pan and add half the butter and the olive oil. Add the spring onions, leeks and garlic and cook for 5 minutes until softened.

■ Add the rice and stir to coat, then tip in the wine and bubble until reduced. Add the stock a little at a time, stirring until the rice is tender with a little bite and oozy. Stir in the parmesan and the rest of butter and season.

Risotto should be oozy, not stiff, so add a splash of stock at the end if you need to.

Tagliatelle with pecorino, lemon and pine nuts

15 minutes ■ Serves 2

tagliatelle 150g
lemon 1, zested and juiced
pine nuts 2 tbsp, toasted
pecorino or **parmesan** 2 tbsp, finely grated
olive oil
parsley a small bunch, chopped

■ Cook the tagliatelle according to the pack instructions.

■ Mix the lemon zest and juice, pine nuts, pecorino or parmesan, 2 tbsp olive oil and the parsley and season really well. Drain the tagliatelle, reserving 2 tbsp of the cooking water. Tip everything into a bowl (including the pasta water) and toss together.

Pecorino is similar in texture to parmesan but has a fresher, saltier flavour.

Aubergine curry with fresh tomato and coriander

20 minutes ■ Serves 4

onion 1, chopped

oil

aubergine 2, sliced into discs

turmeric 1 tsp

ground cumin ½ tsp

ground coriander 1 tsp

nigella seeds 1 tsp

cherry tomatoes 1 punnet

coriander leaves a handful

naan breads and **natural yoghurt** to serve

■ Fry the onion in a slug of oil until soft, then tip onto a plate.

■ Add a little more oil to the pan and fry the aubergine slices in batches until they are browned on each side. Pile the aubergine slices onto a plate as you cook them.

■ Add another slug of oil to the pan and fry the spices for 30 seconds, add back the aubergine and onion, plus the cherry tomatoes, and cook everything together until the cherry tomatoes have burst. Season with salt and scatter with coriander leaves. Serve with naan breads and natural yoghurt or as a side dish with an Indian meal.

Aubergine soaks up masses of oil so don't add too much when frying – as it cooks it will release the oil again.

Stilton and potato pies

45 minutes ■ Serves 4

onions 2, sliced

olive oil

potatoes 4 medium, peeled and parboiled
for 6 minutes, then sliced

Stilton 175g, crumbled

gruyère 100g, coarsely grated

puff pastry 375g, divided into 4 squares

rocket or **watercress** to serve

■ Heat the oven to 200C/fan 180C/gas 6.
Fry the onions in olive oil until soft, then add
the sliced potatoes and toss.

■ Layer the potatoes and the cheeses in
4 individual pie dishes; season with pepper as
you go. Cover each dish with pastry, trim and
crimp the edges and bake for 30–35 minutes
until golden. Serve with the leaves.

If you don't have individual pie dishes
you can build these on small ovenproof
saucers.

Coconut macaroon sandwiches

45 minutes + freezing ■ Makes 12

egg whites 4

golden caster sugar 225g

vanilla extract 1 tsp

ground almonds 2 tbsp

plain flour 2 tbsp

limes 2, zested

shredded sweetened coconut 200g

cream or **strawberry ice cream** and
strawberries for sandwiching

■ Heat the oven to 150C/fan 130C/gas 2. Whisk the egg whites to soft peaks using electric beaters. Slowly add the sugar and vanilla and whisk until combined, then fold in the almonds, flour, lime zest and most of the coconut.

■ Spoon 1½ tablespoon-sized dollops of the batter onto a baking sheet lined with baking paper and spread out. Sprinkle with a pinch of extra coconut and bake for 15 minutes.

■ Remove and cool on the sheet then transfer to a wire rack. Spread a layer of cream or ice cream on a macaroon then top with slivers of strawberry and another macaroon. Freeze for 30 minutes.

Look for shredded coconut in healthfood shops – it has a better flavour than desiccated.

Apple snow

30 minutes ■ Serves 4

egg 2 whites
Bramley apples 500g, peeled, cored and cut into chunks
caster sugar 2–3 tbsp
double cream 284ml carton, softly whipped

■ Whisk the egg whites to stiff peaks. Cook the apples with a splash of water until completely soft, adding enough sugar to sweeten. Cool, then fold in the cream and meringue mixture.

■ Spoon into pretty glasses and chill for 30 minutes.

Bramleys can vary in sharpness so add more or less sugar depending on your fruit.

Peaches with Sauternes panna cotta

25 minutes + setting ■ Serves 6

white or yellow peaches 6, halved and stoned
Sauternes or other dessert wine 2 tbsp
demerara sugar 2 tbsp
PANNA COTTA
sunflower oil
whole milk 300ml
double cream 350ml
caster sugar 100g
gelatine powder 2 tsp, or 4 gelatine leaves soaked in cold water
Sauternes or other dessert wine 75ml

■ To make the panna cotta, brush 4 x 150ml pudding moulds with a little sunflower oil.
■ Put the milk and cream in a pan. Add the sugar, bring slowly to the boil then remove from the heat. Pour 150ml of the milk mix into a small bowl, add the gelatine and stir until it has completely dissolved. Leave the rest of the mixture to cool to room temperature. Stir the 2 mixtures together, add the Sauternes and strain through a fine sieve into the moulds. Chill until set.
■ Heat the oven to 200C/fan 180C/gas 6. Put the peaches in a baking dish, divide the Sauternes between the peaches, pouring it into the holes, and sprinkle over the sugar. Bake for 30 minutes or until the peaches are soft and slightly caramelised. Serve the panna cotta turned out onto plates with the peaches.

White peaches are considered the posh side of the family, but yellow ones work equally well in this recipe.

Strawberry sundae with strawberry sauce

15 minutes + chilling ■ Serves 6

strawberries 18, hulled
golden caster sugar 3 tbsp
orange juice 4 tbsp
double cream 284ml carton
strawberry, **vanilla** and **chocolate**
ice cream
small bananas 6
pecans 50g, toasted and chopped

■ Put 12 of the strawberries in a food processor with 2 tbsp of the sugar and the orange juice. Pulse until coarsely chopped and chill. Softly whip the cream with the remaining sugar. Put a scoop of each flavour of ice cream into 6 bowls and freeze.

■ When ready to serve, chop the remaining strawberries and add to the bowls. Cut the bananas in half lengthways and add these, too. Pour some strawberry sauce over each sundae and finish with a dollop of cream and some nuts.

Orange juice helps bring out the flavour of the strawberries.

Blackberry pavlovas

1 hour 30 minutes ■ Serves 6

eggs 4 whites
golden caster sugar 300g
white vinegar (any type) 2 tsp
cornflour 2 tsp
vanilla extract 1 tsp
blackberries 2 punnets (about 500g)
blackberry or **blackcurrant liqueur** 2 tbsp
(optional)
double cream 284ml carton, whipped

Commercially grown blackberries are
around all summer but the hedgerows
are full of wild ones in September, and
they're free.

■ Heat the oven to 180C/fan 160C/gas 4.

■ Draw 6 small circles on a sheet of baking parchment and put it with the drawn-side down on a baking sheet. Whisk the egg whites until they reach stiff peaks then whisk in 250g sugar in large spoonfuls until you have a stiff, shiny meringue mixture.

■ Whisk in the vinegar, cornflour and vanilla. Dollop the mixture out onto the circles on the parchment and make dips in the centre. Bake for 10 minutes then turn the oven down to 120C/fan 100C/gas ½ for an hour – the meringue should be a very pale biscuit colour. Cool a little, then carefully peel off the paper and put each meringue on a serving plate.

■ While the meringues are cooking, put three-quarters of the blackberries and the rest of the sugar in a pan and cook for a few minutes over a low heat until the blackberries begin to soften and give up their juice and the sugar dissolves.

■ Add the liqueur, if you are using it. Cool, then stir in the uncooked blackberries. Once the meringues are cool, spoon cream into the dips in the centre then spoon over the blackberries.

Vanilla poached pears with butterscotch sauce

30 minutes ■ Serves 4

pears 4 whole, peeled and cored
vanilla pod 1, split
golden caster sugar 150g
butter 30g
light muscovado sugar 100g
golden syrup 2 tbsp
double cream 142ml carton

■ Poach the pears in enough simmering water to cover them, along with the vanilla pod and the caster sugar, for about 15 minutes or until tender. Drain.

■ Simmer the butter, muscovado, golden syrup and double cream for 5–7 minutes until smooth and dark golden.

■ Put the pears in bowls and pour over the butterscotch sauce.

Use ripe but firm pears for this, overripe ones will just turn mushy.

Strawberry zabaglione

30 minutes + chilling ■ Serves 6

eggs 2
golden caster sugar 30g
marsala 2 tbsp
double cream 100ml, softly whipped
strawberries 25, 7 puréed and 18 left whole
small biscuits to serve

■ Put the eggs, sugar, marsala and a pinch of salt in a large glass bowl. Fill another larger bowl with iced water and set aside. Put the first bowl over (not in) a pan of simmering water. Whisk the mixture with electric beaters until very thick or about 3 times the volume.

■ Remove from the heat and set inside the bowl of iced water then whisk again until cold. Fold in the whipped cream and pour into glasses. Swirl a spoonful of the purée through each.

■ Decorate with whole strawberries then chill for at least 3 hours before serving with the biscuits.

Don't over-beat the cream, otherwise combining it with the zabaglione will be difficult. Whisk until it is barely in soft peaks and then gently fold together.

Chocolate orange tart

45 minutes + cooling ■ Serves 8

shortcrust pastry 375g

butter 125g

dark chocolate 200g

eggs 5

golden caster sugar 220g

oranges 2, 1 juiced, both zested

plain flour 70g

cocoa powder to dust

candied peel cut into shreds or pieces
to decorate

■ Heat the oven to 180C/fan 160C/gas 4.
Line a deep 24cm tart tin with the pastry
(roll it as thin as you can). Bake blind for
10 minutes, then remove the paper and
weights. Bake for 10 more minutes.

■ Melt the butter and chocolate. Whisk the
eggs and sugar over a pan of simmering
water until the mixture holds a trail, then fold
in the chocolate mixture, orange juice and
zest, and flour. Pour into the tart case and
bake for 15–20 minutes or until just set. Cool.

■ Dust with cocoa powder and decorate with
slices of candied peel.

**Look for big pieces of candied peel
that you can cut yourself – it has a
better texture and flavour than the
ready-cut stuff.**

Griddled peaches with Amaretto cream

30 minutes ■ Serves 2

peaches 2, halved and stoned
butter
honey
double cream 142ml carton
Amaretto
icing sugar 1 tbsp
flaked almonds, toasted, to serve

■ Heat the oven to 180C/fan 160C/gas 4. Put the peaches cut-side down on a hot griddle (chargrill) for a few minutes until caramelised on the surface. Transfer to a small baking dish, dot with butter and drizzle with honey, then roast for 10–15 minutes until slightly softened (they should still keep their shape).
■ Whip the cream with a splash of Amaretto and the icing sugar. Serve with the peaches. Sprinkle the almonds on top.

You can flavour the cream with whatever liqueur you have – Baileys or Frangelico also work well.

Sweet ricotta pancakes with honey and figs

30 minutes ■ Serves 4

ricotta 250g tub

milk 100ml

flour 75g

baking powder ½ tsp

egg yolks 2

caster sugar 1 tbsp

vanilla extract a few drops

egg whites 2

butter

figs 4 ripe, sliced or quartered to serve

honey to serve

■ Whizz the ricotta, milk, flour, baking powder, egg yolks, sugar and vanilla in a food processer until you have a smooth batter. Whisk the egg whites to stiff peaks and fold into the batter. Heat the butter in a frying pan then drop in spoonfuls of the batter. Cook until golden then flip and cook the other side. Serve with figs and honey to drizzle.

Make sure your figs are really ripe as underripe ones can be woolly and bitter.

Strawberry pancakes with Amaretto syrup and sugared almonds

1 hour ■ Makes 24

SUGARED ALMONDS
whole blanched almonds 50g, roughly chopped
icing sugar 4 tbsp

AMARETTO SYRUP
Amaretto 4 tbsp
maple syrup 150ml

STRAWBERRY PANCAKES
plain flour 250g
golden caster sugar 3 tbsp
baking powder 1½ tsp
butter 3 tbsp, melted
whole milk 350ml
eggs 2, large
oil
vanilla extract ½ tsp
strawberries 200g, cut into thick slices
whipped double cream or **mascarpone** to serve

■ Heat the oven to 180C/fan 160C/gas 4. Put the almonds on a lined baking sheet with the icing sugar and bake for 2 minutes. Shake and put back for 2 minutes. Remove and cool.

■ Bring the Amaretto and maple syrup to a boil. Simmer until thickened then remove from the heat. Reheat it before serving.

■ To make the pancakes, put the dry ingredients in a bowl with a pinch of salt. Pour the wet ingredients into the centre and gently mix. Stir until just combined. Heat a non-stick frying pan until hot. Brush with some oil and pour in 3 small pancakes. When bubbles start appearing, press a strawberry slice into the batter. Turn the pancakes over and brown on the other side.

■ Keep warm in a low oven while you make the others. Serve with sugared almonds, whipped cream or mascarpone, Amaretto syrup and sliced strawberries.

These American-style pancakes are ideal for brunch or pudding. Use a heavy pan for consistent heat while cooking.

Damson cobbler

1 hour ■ Serves 6

damsons 1kg
golden caster sugar 100g
COBBLER
butter 80g, chilled and cut into cubes
self-raising flour 200g
golden caster sugar 100g
buttermilk or **milk** 150ml
hazelnuts or **cobnuts** a handful,
roughly chopped
créme fraîche or **custard**, to serve

■ Heat the oven to 190C/fan 170C/gas 5. Tip the damsons into a 1-litre baking dish and sprinkle over the sugar. Put the dish in the oven while you make the cobbler.

■ To make the cobbler, whizz the butter, flour and sugar and a pinch of salt to fine breadcrumbs in a food processor. Mix in the buttermilk or milk to make very soft, spoonable dough.

■ Take the baking dish out of the oven and spoon blobs of dough over the damsons, sprinkle the cobbler with nuts and bake for 30–35 minutes or until the damson mixture is bubbling and the cobbler is cooked through – test it with a skewer as you would a cake. Serve with crème fraîche or custard.

You won't find damsons in many shops, but you will in farmers' markets and at pick-your-own farms. If you can't find them, just substitute with plums.

Baked stuffed apples with crumble topping

1 hour 10 minutes ■ Serves 6

apples 6 large eating or 6 medium
Bramleys, cores removed
sultanas 50g
cinnamon 1 tsp
butter 75g, chilled
cider 100ml
plain flour 3 tbsp
demerara sugar 4 tbsp
hazelnuts 60g
créme fraîche or **custard**, to serve

■ Heat the oven to 200C/180C/gas 6.
Cut a waist around each apple with a sharp knife so the skin doesn't split when you cook them. Put the apples into a baking dish in which they fit quite snugly.

■ Toss the sultanas with the cinnamon and push them into the holes where the cores were. Add a small knob of butter to each, saving the rest. Pour the cider around and bake for 30 minutes, until the skin is loose.

■ Meanwhile, whizz the flour, sugar and hazelnuts together in a food processor until the nuts are coarsely chopped. Add the rest of the butter in pieces and whizz again to the size of coarse breadcrumbs.

■ When the apples have been cooking for 30 minutes, slip the top piece of skin off each and sprinkle with the crumble mix, pressing it onto each apple. Bake again for 30 minutes. Serve with crème fraîche or custard.

This works equally well with cider or white wine.

Winter berry trifle with caramel shards

30 minutes ■ Serves 8

mixed frozen berries 500g,
defrosted
kirsch or **brandy** 6 tbsp
icing sugar (optional)
trifle sponges 1 pack
mascarpone 250g tub
lemon curd 300g jar
granulated sugar 200g
double cream 284ml carton

■ Mix the berries with kirsch or brandy and sweeten with a little icing sugar if you think they need it. Break as many trifle sponges as will fit in the base of your bowl into short lengths and add them to the berries.

■ Turn them over in the berries with a spoon and then tip the lot into the base of your bowl. Whisk the mascarpone with electric beaters until it gets slightly softer, then fold in the lemon curd. Spoon this on top of the berries, cover with clingfilm and chill until you need it.

■ To make the caramel, put the sugar in a large, heavy-based pan. Put the pan over a low heat and wait until the sugar starts to melt. Tip the pan gently from side to side to help the sugar melt evenly. Once it starts to colour, swirl the pan to keep the colour even and when it has reached a dark gold, dip the base of the pan in cold water to stop it cooking any further.

■ Tip the caramel out onto an oiled baking sheet on a heatproof surface and let it harden and cool. This will keep in an airtight container provided no moisture gets in – if it does the caramel will get sticky.

■ To serve, whip the cream to stiff peaks and dollop it over the surface of the lemon mascarpone. Break the caramel into shards and decorate.

Use a silver-coloured pan when making the caramel – it is much easier to see the colour changing.

Index